YOUR KNOWLEDGE HAS VALUE

- We will publish your bachelor's and master's thesis, essays and papers

- Your own eBook and book - sold worldwide in all relevant shops

- Earn money with each sale

Upload your text at www.GRIN.com
and publish for free

Bibliographic information published by the German National Library:

The German National Library lists this publication in the National Bibliography; detailed bibliographic data are available on the Internet at http://dnb.dnb.de .

This book is copyright material and must not be copied, reproduced, transferred, distributed, leased, licensed or publicly performed or used in any way except as specifically permitted in writing by the publishers, as allowed under the terms and conditions under which it was purchased or as strictly permitted by applicable copyright law. Any unauthorized distribution or use of this text may be a direct infringement of the author s and publisher s rights and those responsible may be liable in law accordingly.

Imprint:

Copyright © 2018 GRIN Verlag
Print and binding: Books on Demand GmbH, Norderstedt Germany
ISBN: 9783668745360

This book at GRIN:

https://www.grin.com/document/428837

Caroline Mutuku

The consequences of the revolution in Iran in the 1970s

GRIN Verlag

GRIN - Your knowledge has value

Since its foundation in 1998, GRIN has specialized in publishing academic texts by students, college teachers and other academics as e-book and printed book. The website www.grin.com is an ideal platform for presenting term papers, final papers, scientific essays, dissertations and specialist books.

Visit us on the internet:

http://www.grin.com/

http://www.facebook.com/grincom

http://www.twitter.com/grin_com

Contents

Introduction 2

Progress of the Pahlavi Dynasty 2

Iranian Revolution and the Setback in the Country's Culture 3

Iranian Relation with the U.S 4

Freedom of Religion in Shah and Islamic State 5

Dictatorship in Islamic State 7

Suppression of Iranians by the Islamic Government 7

Conclusion 8

References 9

Introduction

Iranian revolution of 1979 was believed to be a turning point of the country's struggle for freedom and economic prosperity. Historically, Iran had experienced a series of power transition, especially during the 19th Century. In the early 19th Century, there was a remarkable power shift, which was characterized by a substantial change of leadership styles and developmental strategies. One of the power transitions, which occurred, in the 19th Century was the siege of the Kajar dynasty by Reza Khan, in 1921. Reza Khan overthrew the Kajar dynasty because; he was dissatisfied with the developmental strategies adopted by the Iranian leader. Moreover, the Iranian political regime exercised unprecedented social injustices, especially under the Islamic law. Therefore, Reza overthrew the Kajar dynasty with the principal objective of igniting economic development and social transformation under the wave of western modernization and civilization.

In 1925, Reza Khan established the Pahlevi dynasty after he became the Shah Pahlevi (Northern Virginia Community College, 2011). It was evidenced that the Shah's leadership regime set Iran on a prosperous precedence, especially with regard to the Iranians' freedom and the economic landscape. On the other hand, Iran's international policy enabled it to record tremendous progress in the economy and improvement of the Iranian's living standards. Shah's regime was quite successful compared to the Kajar's and the Khomeini's governments. However, anti-Muslims pressed for the Iranian revolution to reduce the influence of the West and restore Islamic government. The 1979 Iranian revolution was expected to grant Iranians extensive freedom and, enhance economic development. It was also expected to change the country's situation in all aspects. Surprisingly, it appears the revolution did not bear expected outcomes; instead, it reversed economic and social developmental trends at the expense of the Iranians' freedom. The Shah's regime appears to be ideal for Iran's prosperity, although Khomeini discredited its success. Therefore, this research will discuss different ways, in which the Islamic Government has turned the country's social and economic status into unprecedented cascade.

Progress of the Pahlavi Dynasty

The reign of Reza Shah Pahlevi under the Pahlevi dynasty achieved tremendous success compared to the Khomeini's regime. It is worth noting that, Iran experienced immense challenges in communication and transportation in the early 19th Century, especially during the Kajar dynasty. This challenge was addressed by Reza Pahlevi, shortly after he assumed power, in 1921.

Transport and communication systems were established across Iran; thus, promoting economic growth and development (Northern Virginia Community College, 2011). As a result, the living standards of ordinary Iranians improved significantly. However, it is worth noting that the prosperity of the Shah's regime, especially with regard to the country's development could be attributed to the friendly relations, which Reza Shah Pahlevi established with the Axis powers; the United States of America and Britain during the post World War I. The pro-Allied policy was also adopted by Reza's son, Muhammad Reza Shah Pahlevi who succeeded him and maintained his developmental strategies.

Another remarkable success of the Shah's regime was the tremendous growth of the oil industry, which sparked Iran's economic development and propelled it to success, in the Middle East. It is worth noting that the flourishing of the oil industry was facilitated by the establishment of efficient transport and communication networks. In addition, Western countries, especially Britain and the U.S played a significant role to the rapid development of the oil industry by providing market for crude oil. The U.S and European countries relied heavily on oil imports from Iran and, this is probably the reason as to why Britain and the Soviet Union rushed to protect oil fields, in 1941, in the effort of blocking Germany from assuming control over oil production, in Iran. As a result, Iran laws, which allowed foreign, oil companies to control the oil industry, in Iran (Northern Virginia Community College, 2011).

Moreover, the Shah's regime introduced Westernization program, which transformed the country's social landscape by introducing Western civilization among Muslims. The ultimate benefits of Westernization were freedom of religious and the adoption of a modern lifestyle, which improved the Iranian's quality of life. However, the Shah experienced unprecedented political crisis, especially in 1950s, which prompted for the prime minister's eminence through extraordinary powers (January, 2008).

Iranian Revolution and the Setback in the Country's Culture

Concisely, the Iranian revolution of 1979 was spearheaded by Ayatollah Ruhollah Khomeini who had initiated the struggle for the establishment of an Islamic republic. Khomeini was a prominent Shiite Muslim Clergyman who had been exiled to France, in 1963 whose return to Iran, in 1979 sparked widespread riots, in Iran. As a result, the Shah fled the country owing to immense opposition; thus, Khomeini established an Islamic Republic governed by Islamic law, in 1979. Thereafter, Khomeini reversed the Westernization culture, which had been established by the Shah's regime. He also ended the country's friendly relationship with the U.S, especially after the capture of 66 Americans in Teheran's U.S embassy by Iranian militants on 4th November 1979 (Digital History, 2013).

From an analytical perspective, Khomeini's government led to the unprecedented setback of the country's culture, owing to the introduction of the Islamic laws (Hurd, 2009). Iranians had adopted western civilization and incorporated the Western way of life into their cultural practices. In addition, most Iranians, especially the non-Shiite Muslims had abandoned some oppressive Islamic laws, which denied them freedom. However, followers of the conservative Shiite Islam maintained the most principal elements of the Islamic culture.

Westernization, which allowed Iranians to choose their way of life, outside the cords of Islamic law enhanced efficient social development among the Iranian population. Some of the benefits of the Western civilization among Iranians included women empowerment and the reduction of social inequalities. In contrast, the Islamic Republic abolished Westernization by enforcing Islamic law. The people's social life is governed by the tenets of Islam, which give men dominance over women; thus, enhancing gender inequality in the society (Povey & Rostami-Povey 2).

However, virtually all the cultural changes, which occurred during the Shah's regime, were reversed after the revolution because; the Islamic Republic re-introduced the Islamic law, which forced the alienated Iranians to shun the life-transforming Western culture for the ordinary uncivilized way of living under the Islamic law. Therefore, it is blatantly true to assert that the 1979's revolt seems to have set the country's culture back a decade.

Iranian Relation with the U.S

Iran's political revolutionary changes seem to have interfered with the country's foreign policy. In the early 1920s, especially during the Kajar dynasty, Iran did not have reliable links with foreign countries. In addition, its relationship with its neighbors, in the Middle East was highly strained. However, Reza Shah Pahlevi established friendly relations with the Western countries, which enhanced the country's progress in all aspects of development.

The Shah's relationship with the United States is believed to as one of the most principal factors, which enabled Iran to advance economically, especially with regard to rapid development of infrastructure and the oil industry. Reza Pahlevi adopted a pro-Allied policy, in which the U.S became its developmental partner through the exchange of imports and exports. It is believed that the observed economic retardation, which followed shortly after the establishment of the Islamic Republic, in 1979, can be attributed to the strained relationship between Khomeini's regime and the United States.

At first, Iranian militants ambushed the U.S embassy, in Teheran, in 1979 after the U.S allowed the ousted Shah to receive medical treatment, in the United States. By doing so, Khomeini wanted to pressurize the U.S to handover the Shah to his government for prosecution on alleged laundering of Iran's revenue (Northern Virginia Community College, 2011). The retention of the 53 hostages by Iran angered President Carter's Administration; thus, prompting the U.S to resort to a military approach to rescue the hostages from the Iranian authorities, in 1981.

However, Iran's relationship with the U.S turned into enmity after it expressed intense opposition to Israel policies, in Palestine. Iran portrays unfriendly relationship with the foreign countries, especially with regard to its perception on the presence of Israel, in the Middle East. Iran has been fueling strife between Israel and Palestine through according military assistance to Hezbollah and the Hamas regime. This has led to the introduction of economic sanctions against the Iranian Government by the U.S because; it is a diplomatically to Israel and, this has derailed the country's economic progress. In contrast, the 1979 revolution was expected to extend Iran's relationship with foreign countries as it was the case with the Shah's regime. Concisely, the Islamic Government led to the unprecedented disconnect between Iran and the foreign countries. It has failed to foster peaceful relationship with the international community and, this aspect was evidenced in 1980 when Iran got into a conflict with Iraq, leading to the unprecedented disruption of the country's economy after its oil production declined significantly. This was occasioned by Iraq's capture of Khuzestan and Shatt al Arab provinces, which are known to be endowed with vast oil resources (Northern Virginia Community College, 2011).

Freedom of Religion in Shah and Islamic State

Freedom of religion, in Iran, seems to have lost its significance, shortly, after the Pahlevi dynasty collapsed and allowed Khomeini to establish an Islamic Republic. It is believed that the Shah had made remarkable advances towards upholding freedom rights of the Iranians. He allowed Iranians to choose their religious denominations and, this was attributable to the Shah's Westernization approaches in which he permitted Christianity to penetrate into his dynasty. Shah's embarked on Westernization of Iran to pave the way for a modern revolution by introducing land, economic and social reforms, in 1963 (BBC, 2013). As a result, the wave of Westernization attracted Christian denominations in the predominant Muslim population. There were also other religious minorities, which included the Jews and the Zoroastrians. From an analytical perspective, the Shah did not resist religious reforms owing to his approaches of Westernization and, this is probably the reason as to why the conservative Shiite Muslims responded violently to the Shah's regime.

Despite the vehement resistance from radical Muslims, the Iranian population enjoyed an unprecedented freedom of worship. The Pahlevi dynasty seemed relatively different from the earlier monarchial dynasties, which upheld the Islamic law in all aspects of leadership. Therefore, the Shah is regarded to be one of the most significant personalities, in Iran who granted people their fundamental rights and freedoms.

In contrast, the re-establishment of the Islamic Republic by Khomeini, in 1979, in which he declared Shi'ism a state religion seems to have taken away the Iranians' freedom of religion. This is probably so because; the Shah's authoritarian regime did not force Iranians to uphold Islam but, it allowed them to chose their preferred religion. Moreover, the Shah's regime was less concerned with the enforcement of religious doctrines; instead religious leaders of various religious were the stewards of their religions. Therefore, the Pahlevi dynasty did not have an established state religion.

On the other hand, the Khomeini's administration introduced an authoritarian Islamic regime, in which Islamic laws were applied in all aspects of social and economic issues. It is reported, "Khomeini exercised enormous influence and imposed a strict set of Islamic laws that banned informal contact between unrelated men and women, forced women to cover their heads and bodies in public" (Democracy Web, 2010 par. 7). This was contrary to the Shah's perception on the freedom of women and, this was evidenced by his remarks, "Women are free in the Islamic Republic in the selection of their activities and their future and their clothing" (Isseroff, 2009 par. 21). Moreover, the Shah's monarchy had granted women substantial freedom but, all that was eroded under the Khomeini's regime. Kar (2010) remarks, "Iranian women lost the rights they had acquired in the last decade of Pahlavi monarchy" (par. 1). He further states that the status of the Iranian women has experienced immense deterioration during the Islamic regime compared to the pre-revolution period, in which the Shah reigned (Kar, 2010). The harsh environment of the authoritarian Islamic regime was evidenced by the fleeing of 50, 000 Jews from Iran.

Dictatorship in Islamic State

Moreover, the Islamic Republic transformed what was supposed to be an anti-dictatorial popular revolution based on a broad coalition of all anti-Shah forces quickly transformed into an Islamic fundamentalist power-grab. Khomeini became the supreme leader and he was bestowed with appointing all principal heads of the governmental agencies. A report from the Democracy Web (2010) states, "The supreme leader has vaguely worded supervisory powers over all parts of government, and during his period of rule" (par. 7).

Ironically, the anti-shah radicals claimed to fight for a secular-free State, in which Iranians would be set free from the cords dictatorship but, Khomeini's regime took away the people's freedom and subjected them into oppressive authoritarian Islamic leadership. Currently, the authoritarian Islamic Government continues to interfere with the Iranians way of life in virtually all aspects of social being. The Islamic regime has subjected the Iranian people to unfathomable brutality because; the intolerant regime does not give attention to the voice of its people. As a result, Iranians are deprived of their right to contribute significantly to their future, especially through decision making.

Suppression of Iranians by the Islamic Government

It is believed that the Islamic regime has further suppressed Iranians by introducing unrealistic educational system and, perpetrating social injustices, especially in the 1980s.
Shortly after Khomeini seized power from the Shah, the Islamic regime established inefficient educational system through which Islam is perpetrated. For instance, Iran's educational textbooks and other learning materials contain bias information, especially with regard to religion. They contain Islamic teachings and fictional propaganda about the Islamic Government; thus, the educational system exhibit unprecedented social inequalities.

On the other hand, the Islamic regime has been subjecting Iranians to enormous social injustices. However, the Shah's regime portrayed injustices by exercising the brutal killing of protesters and revolutionaries who were involved in the 1978-1979 revolt, the Khomeini's regime cause immense bloodshed by seizing power with violence.

Currently, the Iranian president exercises excessive dictatorship and, those who seem to challenge his leadership are locked up in prison. For instance, women activists fighting for their social rights have been subjected to unfathomable brutality. Kar (2010) reports, "Currently, many courageous Iranian women, who have supported the protesting national movement, are in prison" (par. 1). Coughlin (2009) also unearths dictatorship, in Iran by saying, "Cries of "Death to the Shah" have now been replaced by regular chants of "Death to the Dictator", a reference to [the] hard-line President, Mahmoud Ahmadinejad" (par. 3).

Conclusion

In a brief conclusion, it is evident that the revolution in 1979 and the rise of the Islamic republic gave Iran its independence and suspended the westernization process, leading to the current situation characterized with social injustices and economic retardation. From an analytical perspective, the Iranian revolution seems to have presented an unprecedented setback to civilization owing to the resurgence of Islam. It is worth noting that the Pahlevi dynasty had established efficient economic and social reforms, which could have propelled Iran to auspicious success. Unfortunately, the benefits of Westernization and modernity seem to have been foregone with the establishment of the so-called revolutionized Iranian Government because: revolution meant different things to different groups of revolutionaries and it followed the path towards making Iran worse rather than better.

References

BBC (2013, April 9). *Iran Profile* [Press Release]. Retrieved from http://www.bbc.co.uk/news/world-middle-east-14542438

Coughlin, C. (2009, June 15). *Iran Analysis: Protest Draws Comparisons with 1979 Revolution* [Press Release]. Retrieved from http://www.telegraph.co.uk/news/5543261/Iran-analysis-protest-draws-comparisons-with-1979-revolution.html

Democracy Web (2010). *The Consent of the Governed: Country Studies - Islamic Republic of Iran.* Retrieved from http://www.democracyweb.org/consent/iran.php

Digital History (2013). *Teheran Students Seize U.S Embassy And Hold Hostages: Ask Shah's Return And Trial.* Retrieved from http://www.digitalhistory.uh.edu/disp_textbook.cfm?smtID=3&psid=1173

Hurd, E. (2009). *The Politics of Secularism in International Relations.* Princeton, NJ: Princeton University Press.

Isseroff, A. (2009). *Encyclopedia of the Middle East; Ayatollah Ruhollah Khomeini.* Retrieved from http://www.mideastweb.org/Middle-East-Encyclopedia/ayatollah_khomeini.htm

January, B. (2008). *The Iranian Revolution.* Minneapolis, MN: Twenty-First Century Books Publishing.

Kar. M. (2010). *Women, the Victims of the Iranian Revolution.* Retrieved from http://www.gozaar.org/english/articles-en/Women-the-Victims-of-the-Iranian-Revolution.html

Northern Virginia Community College (2011). *1979 Iranian Revolution.* Retrieved from http://novaonline.nvcc.edu/eli/evans/his135/Events/Iran79.htm

Povey, T., & Rostami-Povey, E. (2012). *Women, Power and Politics in Twenty-first Century Iran.* Farnham, UK: Ashgate Publishing, Ltd.

YOUR KNOWLEDGE HAS VALUE

- We will publish your bachelor's and master's thesis, essays and papers

- Your own eBook and book -
  sold worldwide in all relevant shops

- Earn money with each sale

Upload your text at www.GRIN.com and publish for free